Powerful Passages

A selection of short devotional articles

Compiled and Edited

By Michael Penny

ISBN: 978-1-78364-619-7

www.obt.org.uk

****

THE OPEN BIBLE TRUST
Fordland Mount, Upper Basildon,
Reading, RG8 8LU, UK

Powerful Passages

Contents

Introduction

These devotional articles first appeared on the pages of *Search* magazine over a number of years, many of which were written by Cliff Richmond, one of the founding trustees of The Open Bible Trust.

It has been my pleasure to compile them, but they have required very little editing, and I am indebted to Karen Abbotts. It was her idea to pull them all together and publish them in a book. She also typed them from the pages of the back issues of *search* and put them into one electronic file – which made my job so much easier.

The prayer of both Karen and myself is that readers will find this collection a helpful blessing

Michael Penny

Genesis 1

Cliff Richmond

There are many powerful passages in the Bible, in both the Old and New Testaments. Those that come to my mind more than any others are all in Genesis 1. I think the whole chapter, from beginning to end, reveals and radiates the power of God.

It is rather difficult to put into words exactly what I feel, but when I read through it, I somehow have a mental picture of the beginning – nothing but absolute darkness on an enormous and imaginable scale (verse 2).

Then God said, 'Let there be light'. There was light and we have day and night (verse 5). And so it continues. The firmament called heaven (verse 7); the dry land (verse 9); grass, herbs and fruit trees (verses 11-12); lights in the heaven (verses 14-15); then two great lights and the stars (verse 16).

God ordered the waters to bring forth abundantly the moving creature that has life. He created fowl that fly above the earth (verse 20). He made every living creature: cattle and creeping thing and beast of the earth.

Then God said, 'Let us make man.' And it was so. Male and female created He them. This, I think is gloriously powerful reading!

When I sit down and relax, then read the chapter slowly and really think about what I am reading, I can imagine it all happening.

Commencing with the blackness of nothing, changes take place as God uses His divine power to bring into being that which He desires.

For me, the biblical words invoke breathtaking awe. Then an indescribable sense of His Will and power comes across me, almost like a physical feeling.

As I now live in the country-side, I have more opportunities to see the result of our God's creation than I did when living in London. Every day, as I look out of my window, I am reminded of Genesis 1 and the power who is behind it all.'

I would like to thank Mrs. de Vries for drawing our attention to this truly *powerful passage*. Her comments add to its majesty.

Genesis 1 deals with God's physical creation, but there is another, a spiritual one. In 2 Corinthians 5:17 Paul states, 'If anyone is in Christ, he is a new creation.' A closer examination of Genesis 1 reveals some interesting parallels between God's original physical creation and His new creation in those who have put their faith in Christ.

As space is restricted, I can only give the bare bones and leave the reader to seek further.

(1) **A state of disorder**
  - **Genesis 1:2**
    a) Confusion: no order, nothing, in harmony with God's ultimate purpose, nothing perfect. (Romans 8:5-8; Titus 3:3)

b) Emptiness: void, unable to produce anything good (Ecclesiastes 1:1-4; 2:1-11). Life and fruitfulness are gifts of God (Romans 7:18; Job 14:1-4).

c) Darkness: until light is sent forth (2 Corinthians 4:6). Satan is the prince of darkness; Jesus is the light of the world.

(2) **The work of the Spirit**
- **Genesis 1:2**

The Spirit moved. The earth's own movement could not put right the state of disorder. The same is true of us. We need to be moved by the Spirit. (John 3:3; 1:12-13; 6:63; Titus 3:4-6)

(3) **The powerful word of God**
- **Genesis 1:3, 6, 9, 11, 14, 20, 24, 26, 29**

The word of God is quick and powerful (Hebrews 4:12) and this word is the Gospel of Christ (Romans 1:17). His word is with power (John 11:43).

(4) **Divine separation**
- **Genesis 1:4-5**

The Holy Spirit working in us sanctifies (2 Corinthians 6:14-7:1).

(5) **Bearing fruit**
- **Genesis 1:11**

This is the effect of the light and the moving of the Spirit. The fruit of Christ in us will be Christ likeness (Matthew 7:16-20; Colossians 1:6).

(6) **The position of the lights**
- **Genesis 1:15**

They are above the earth and are to shine out. So, too, should we (Matthew 5:14-16; John 17:16; Ephesians 2:6-7; Colossians 3:1-2).

(7) **The image of God**
- **Genesis 1:27**

The climax of His creative power is in His own image. (Colossians 3:9-10; 1 John 3:1-2). God and man satisfied (Genesis 1:31).

(8) **A position of honour**
   - **Genesis 1:28**
   Rule over them (2 Timothy 2:11-12).

Does this outline reflect our own life story – from darkness to light; from death to life? If not, then let the Word of God and His Holy Spirit move and work in our hearts. Let us pray to the Father and trust in the Lord Jesus for forgiveness and eternal life.

Psalm 22

His sufferings and glory

Cliff Richmond

This prophetic Psalm sets forth the Messiah as the Good Shepherd (John 10:11), and forms a group, with Psalms 23 and 24, which point to the Messiah as The Great Shepherd (Hebrews 13:20) and the Chief Shepherd (1 Peter 5:4).

The Psalm splits into two parts: verses 1-21 deal with the Messiah's sufferings while verses 22-31 show His glory. The Psalm must be prophetic of Christ. It cannot be dealing with the sufferings of David. Who 'pierced his hands and feet'? Who 'parted his garments and cast lots upon his vesture'?

Verses 1, 7, 8, 14, 16 and 18 are all familiar to us as they appear in the New Testament accounts of our Lord's crucifixion. Death by crucifixion is vividly described in this Psalm, yet this form of punishment had not been devised when David wrote. It was not used until centuries later, by the Romans.

Christ's suffering on the cross is a unique event, that will never need repeating. A sinless man – Himself God manifest in flesh – was made sin (2 Corinthians 5:21), and so He was forsaken of God (Psalm 22:1-2) because 'He was made a curse for us' (Galatians 3:13).

As well as being forsaken by God, Psalm 22:6 describes him as 'a worm and not a man, scorned and despised by the people'. *The*

Companion Bible notes that the Hebrew word for worm is 'not the ordinary word but the crimson *coccus* from which the scarlet dye was obtained'. The word is rendered scarlet in Exodus 25:4; 26:1. This again, is prophetic of Christ's blood shed on the cross.

It is also to be noted that the suffering from the reproach and scorn of wicked men was compounded since it was for these men that He suffered. In verses 7 and 8 He is derided by those who mocked His faith in God as being in vain. They laugh at His weakness as evidence of failure yet it is for such as these that He died!

In verse 14 we read, 'I am poured out like water', showing how He emptied Himself and became of no reputation, pouring His soul out unto death and giving all that He had. The Hymn *And Can It Be* contains the lines 'Emptied Himself of all but love and bled for Adam's helpless race'.

Verse 15 shows us His humiliation 'Thou hast brought me unto the dust of death'. This was His own voluntary humility whereby 'the Good Shepherd lays His life for the sheep' (John 10:11). 'He humbled Himself and became obedient to death even death on a cross' (Philippians 2:8).

This death involved being nailed to a cross. 'They pierced my hands and my feet' (Psalm 22:16). Thus the Lord of Glory was crucified, and death on a cross was the most painful and shameful of all deaths. 'He endured the cross scorning its shame' (Hebrews 12:2). 'He suffered for us, the Just for the unjust that He might bring us to God' (1 Peter 3:18).

Psalm 22:22-31

Cliff Richmond

In our previous study of this Psalm (His Sufferings and Glory) we looked at verses 1-21 which dealt with the Messiah's sufferings. We are now concerned with verses 22-31 which show His glory. There are many references in the first part of the Psalm to Christ suffering the death of crucifixion. However, in the second section reference is made to His resurrection and future reign.

Verse 22, "I will declare your name to my *brothers*, in the congregation I will praise you," is quoted in Hebrews 2:12 as being the Lord's words in resurrection. Confirmation of this is found in John 20:17 when he told Mary Magdalene, "Do not hold on to me, for I have not yet returned to the Father. Go instead to my *brothers* and tell them, "I am returning to my Father and your Father, to my God and to your God,'" and in 1 Corinthians 15:6 where we read, "after that he appeared to more than five hundred of the *brothers* at the same time." So the Name of the Lord was "declared to my *brothers*, in the congregation."

Verse 23 continues the theme of praise to the Lord and in the words of Philippians 2:9-11 we see again the relationship of the sufferings and glory. "Therefore," because of His sufferings and death on a cross, "God exalted Him to the highest place and gave Him the name that is above every name, that at the name of Jesus every knee should bow, in heaven and on earth and under the earth, and every tongue confess that Jesus Christ is Lord, to the glory of God the Father."

In verse 24 we see that "the suffering of the afflicted one" was not ignored by His Father and His cry for help was not in vain.

We see in verse 26 the assurance of His grace; "the poor will eat and be satisfied." Do we acknowledge day by day that His grace is sufficient for us? As Isaiah said, "Listen, listen to me, and eat what is good, and your soul will delight in the richest of fare" (Isaiah 55:2). In His future kingdom it is likely that the meek (poor) of verse 26 are the rich (prosperous or fat) of verse 29 – see Psalm 36:8, 63:5.

Verse 29 may mean that they, and all who like them were doomed to return to the dust because of sin, will praise Him, because in order to save them, He did not keep alive His own soul.

In these latter verses Messiah's glory is evidenced by the triumph of His cause as "all the ends of the earth will remember and turn to the Lord . . . for dominion belongs to the Lord and He rules over the nations."

Zechariah 14:9 is to the point here; "The Lord (once the rejected king) will be the king over the whole earth. On that day there will be one Lord, and His name the only name." So, too, is Revelation 11:15 where we read, "The kingdom of the world has become the kingdom of our Lord and of His Christ, and He will reign for ever and ever."

So let us remember that He died for us, that He might be Lord both of the living and the dead and may we "proclaim His righteousness . . . for He has done it" verse 31, - the last phrase being equivalent to "it is finished," the Lord's words on the cross. A perfect end to this perfect portion of the perfect *Law of the Lord*.

Psalm 33:1-12

Rejoice in the Lord

Cliff Richmond

Rejoice in the Lord was dealt with earlier this year by Willie Henry and Peter Mansell, the speakers at the OBT Nottingham Conference which provided us with lessons from Philippians. It is rightly called the epistle of joy because rejoice or rejoicing occurs nine times in its four chapters. The equivalent book in the Old Testament must be Psalms where these words occur over 60 times.

'Rejoice in the Lord' is how verse 1 of Psalm 33 is rendered in the *KJV* but other translations give the more powerful 'Shout for joy in the Lord!'. It is to be noted that the righteous are told to do this shouting because 'it is fitting for the upright to praise Him'. This opening verse is connected to the last verse of the previous Psalm which also has 'rejoice in the Lord' and adds 'be glad'.

In verse 3 they are told to 'sing to Him a *new* song'. Could this be because they have been made *new* creatures (see 2 Corinthians 5:17)? This *new* song is a hymn of praise to God (Psalm 40:3) and has been put in the mouths of those lifted out of the slimy pit, the mud and mire and instead, have been given a firm place to stand. Singing a new song is the theme of many other Psalms – see, for example, 46:1, 98:1, 144:9, 149:1 and also Isaiah 42:10.

In the book of Revelation we are told the words of a new song (Revelation 5:9-13) – a song of praise to the Lord for redeeming men by His blood. In Revelation 14:3 we are told that 'no one could learn the song except the 144,000 who had been redeemed from the earth.'

But what of ourselves? What is the source of our joy? Is it in the world? in ourselves? – or in the Lord Jesus because He has made us righteous by redeeming us through His death on the cross and has made us new creatures? If this is the case, then as believers we have something to shout about. As someone once remarked 'it is good to leave the doubters and join the shouters!'

Psalm 33 goes on to mention other things which should make believers rejoice in the Lord.

(1) **His word and works (vs 4-7)**

What He says is right and true and He is faithful in all He does. Some people habitually tell lies and it can be difficult to know when they can be trusted or relied upon but with God's word we know we can depend on it for it is the truth (John 17:17).

(2) **His unfailing love (v 5 *NIV*)**

I am reminded of the hymn of G. W. Robinson which begins:

> Loved with everlasting love
> Led by grace that love to know.

The second verse is:

> Heaven above is softer blue,
> Earth around is sweeter green
> Something lives in every hue,

Christless eyes have never seen:
Birds with gladder song o'erflow
Flowers with deeper beauties shine,
Since I know as now I know,
I am His and He is mine.

Yes! The Christian can see that the earth is full of the Lord's loving kindness (v 5 *RV*) whereas others may not have the eyes to see. It is true that God 'makes the sun to rise on the evil and on the good and sends rain on the just and the unjust' (Matthew 5:45). Thus He cares for even those who do not see Him and His creation.

(3) His power (vs 8-9)

God is love and He showed the depth of that love when He sent His one and only Son into the world that we might live through Him. Men can deny the word of God but such is His power that nothing can separate believers from the love that is in Christ Jesus our Lord. So the psalmist can say 'How happy is the nation whose God is the Lord, the people he chooses for his inheritance' (v 12). Therefore how happy we should be. Let us rejoice in the Lord. Let us sing joyfully to the Lord. Let us shout for joy!

Isaiah 40:31

Christina Miller and Cliff Richmond

The powerful passage in this issue of *Search* has been contributed by Christina Miller of Ipswich. We are grateful to her and she writes about Isaiah 40:31.

"As I grow in the Christian life I experience many problems, but I also find how faithful God is . . . and how faithless I am.

There are so many times when confused and troubled by problems, I try to work them out by myself. Instead of turning to God and letting Him take over, I turn away from Him.

The harder I try to find a solution, the more confused I become. The results are disastrous. I become tired and weak, both physically and spiritually, growing further and further away from Him, the source of all truth, goodness and love.

It can produce also physical illness, as I have found to my cost. Days, perhaps weeks, of feeling unwell until suddenly, weak and helpless, I hear a still, small voice calling to me. I fall to my knees in prayer and, confessing my sin, turn back to God who waits for me to ask Him for help.

What a difference when I wait upon the Lord, turning my problem over to Him. How my strength returns, along with a deep peace within. There is a wonderful feeling of well-being, knowing that everything will be alright because He is in control.

It is through these trials and troubles that with new insight I look again at Isaiah 40:31, especially the words 'Those who wait upon the Lord gain new strength'. This verse speaks to me, revealing its truth.

Although we may turn from God, he never turns away from us. He is always there, speaking to us in that still small voice and waiting for us to, once again, wait upon Him and gain new strength."

In Job 22:21 the words of Eliphaz are helpful: 'Acquaint thyself with Him, and be at peace'. A theoretical knowledge of God cannot satisfy the heart, but acquaintance implies a personal intimacy.

Adam, through sin, separated himself from God and Divine friendship had to be set up on a new basis, one of faith. Nowadays no one can be acquainted with God if they are a stranger to the Lord Jesus Christ Who was God manifest in the flesh and Who has made peace for us by His death on the cross.

The way back to fellowship with God is stated in Job 22:22-23, 'Receive!' 'Repent!' Receive what He has said in His word about sin and salvation. Return to Him by yielding ourselves (our will) to Him.

Verse 23 continues: 'You shall be built up'. When we come into the light of His presence we are rebuilt, we are made new creatures. 'If any man be in Christ he is a new creature' wrote Paul in 2 Corinthians 5:17.

Job 22:24-26 tells us that 'The Almighty shall be our treasure' (*RV*) and that we will find our delight in Him. The gold of Ophir is but the dust of the earth when compared to the riches that are in Him.

To know God is to be a spiritual millionaire for He 'has blessed us in the heavenly realms with every spiritual blessing in Christ' and in the coming ages He is going to show us 'the incomparable riches of His grace' (Ephesians 1:3; 2:7).

Matthew 27:27-44

Cliff Richmond

Then the governor's soldiers took Jesus into the Praetorium and gathered the whole company of soldiers around Him. They stripped Him and put a scarlet robe on Him, and then wove a crown of thorns and set it on His head. They put a staff in His right hand and knelt in front of Him and mocked Him. "Hail, king of the Jews!" they said. They spat on Him, and took the staff and struck Him on the head again and again. After they had mocked Him, they took off the robe and put His own clothes on him. Then they led him away to crucify him ... Two robbers were crucified with Him, one on His right and one on His left. Those who passed by hurled insults at Him, shaking their heads and saying, "You who are going to destroy the temple and build it in three days, save yourself! Come down from the cross, if you are the Son of God!"

In the same way the chief priests, the teachers of the law and the elders mocked Him. "He saved others," they said, "but He can't save himself! He's the King of Israel! Let him come down now from the cross, and we will believe in Him. He trusts in God. Let God rescue him now if He wants Him, for He said, 'I am the Son of God.'" In the same way the robbers who were crucified with Him also heaped insults on Him.

The above verses are part of the account of the Crucifixion and the events leading up to it. The force of these words really struck me a few years ago during a church service I was leading. My sermon was based on the passage which I read to the congregation.

By the time I reached verse 30 my emotions prevented me from continuing. After a pause to wipe away the tears and encouraged by whispers of 'Bless Him!', I struggled to the end of the reading.

Why was I thus affected? I saw my Saviour stripped, spat on and struck by the soldiers. But there was more. My Master was mocked and murdered by a malicious mob. All this for what? For me!

Consider for a moment those involved in this sad scene.

(1) The soldiers representing the military rulers.
(2) Those who passed by – just ordinary people.
(3) The chief priests, teachers of the law and the elders, who represented the spiritual rulers.
(4) The robbers who were crucified with Him and who were justly condemned common criminals.

All these different types of people heaped insults on the Son of God. At any moment He could have exercised His power as God and come down off the Cross. But he chose not to. He chose death. He died not for His own sins, but for ours.

There was another occasion when He refused to work miracles for Himself, when tempted by the devil in the wilderness. Many Christians think of this self-denial during Lent, the weeks leading up to Easter. Often things are given up in Lent, but the greatest thing given up was at Easter, when our Lord Jesus Christ offered up Himself. By giving up His life He chose to save others and not Himself. What a demonstration of His love towards us!

Mark 13:32

Rev. D. C. Porter and Cliff Richmond

'Of that day and that hour knows no man, no, not the angels which are in heaven, neither the Son, but the Father.'

In Appendix 2 of his book *Signs of the Second Coming[1]*, Michael Penny discussed Matthew 24:36, a verse parallel to Mark 13:32 quoted above. The following article from Rev. D. C. Porter was received prior to the publication of that book.

'Mark 13:32 has always been regarded as a difficult verse to expound, especially in the light of the Eternal Sonship and the omniscience that is characteristic of the Divine Nature. One explanation has been to emphasise the humbleness of mind in the Saviour, who chose not to draw upon infinite resources of His omniscience, whilst living the life of an obedient Servant.

During my recent tour of India and Nepal, I was privileged to stay at The Leprosy Hospital, Anandaban. One of the staff members had a sister who was getting married. They were a Brahman family – a high priestly caste in the Hindu religion. To me was extended an invitation to the engagement celebrations taking place in the house of the bride to be.

[1] Published by The Open Bible Trust.

On arrival at the Nepali house, I was introduced to the prospective bride, when the customary **namasdae** greetings were exchanged. Then everyone present enjoyed the Nepali meal that had been prepared.

My curiosity was aroused by the notable absence of the bridegroom. He had been at the house on the previous day, when the couple had been formally engaged. Now, while we were rejoicing with the bride, he was at home gathering around him his processional party and musical companions.

My American missionary friend then intimated to me that she just received an invitation to witness the actual Brahman wedding, taking place the following day. "What time is it due to take place?" I enquired. "Why, no one knows that except the high priest", my friend replied. "Well, how can they organise the provisions and time the arrangements unless they know the actual moment of the ceremony?" was my reply. "They must all keep themselves in diligent readiness, 'of course," she replied.

Apparently, whilst the bridegroom is at home gathering his friends, and the bride and her family and friends are in constant expectancy, the high priest will be studying the stars.

A signal will not be relayed to the bridegroom to move towards his bride until the high priest is assured that the blessings of the heavens will be upon the marriage.

Once the high priest sees constellation relativity, then a message is sent to the bridegroom. Hastily his party will assemble, headed by a band of musicians. The trumpeters will sound out the news that the bridegroom is coming for his bride.

We can be assured that the Father knows the precise moment of the Coming of our Lord. When things in heaven and things on earth are just right, then the Father will signal the Son of God, Who will come and receive His Bride.

The Apostle John foresaw signs in heaven (Revelation 15:1) before the joyous announcement that the marriage of the Lamb is come (Revelation 19:7). Like the high priest in the Brahman ceremony, so the Father alone knows just when the signal is to be relayed to the Bridegroom. Then the "trumpet shall sound", and those believers who have been kept in diligent readiness will know what the clarion notes signify – Christ is coming for His saints, who are arrayed in fine linen, clean and white (Revelation 19:8).'

We are grateful to Rev. Porter of the Leprosy Mission for this further light on the Lord's words. While the Brahman wedding guests 'must keep themselves in diligent readiness', so the members of the Church which is the Body of Christ must 'live self-controlled, upright and godly lives in this present age, *while we wait for the blessed hope – the glorious appearing* of our great God and Saviour, Jesus Christ, who gave himself for us to redeem us from all wickedness and to purify for himself a people that are his very own, eager to do what is good'. (Titus 2:12-14).

John 9:25

'Whereas I was blind, now I see!'

John Bent and Cliff Richmond

My own definition of a *powerful passage* is one that when I read it, or heard it read in church, it had an effect on me that was *electric*. Alternatively, one particular verse may be remembered because it brought great comfort at a time of need, or we sensed it to be God's guidance through a crisis.

Sometimes in a church service, people may give their testimonies, by relating their conversion experience or how the Lord has continued to work in their life. Mr. John Bent of Chester would like to share his story with readers, explaining how John 9:25 is a *Powerful Passage* for him.

Billy Graham visited this country in 1955, conducting his crusade in Kelvin Hall. I decided to go to hear him at Central Hall, Liverpool, where his meetings were being relayed. The date was the 22nd April 1955. When it came time for him to make his appeal he asked everyone to bow their heads and pray for the persons sitting next to them. I bowed my head and thought I was alright, there was no need for me to go forward, but it was as if someone said, 'Are you sure?' The next thing I remember was being out in the gangway and going forward. After that I felt lifted up.

The outcome was that on the following Monday evening three days after my wonderful experience, there was a knock on our door which I answered. Standing there was an old gentleman from Rainhill Methodist Church – I lived in Rainhill then.

He told me that the Tuesday Devotional Service was short of someone to conduct it and would I do it? I had never done anything like that in my life before and if that request had been put to me four days before I would have wanted the ground to open and swallow me up. Instead my answer was that I would do it.

The following day I conducted that service and preached without notes as I hadn't really had the time to prepare for the service.

A few days later a local preacher from that church met me and said he had heard about me. He asked if I would like to become a local preacher. Then he told me not to answer him then, but to pray about it and let him know the outcome. That night I prayed about it and was convinced that it was God's will that I should answer in the affirmative.

Several days later I met this gentleman again and I told him the answer was 'Yes! I would like to study and to become a local preacher, that I felt it was God's wish'. Then he said he had felt led to ask me and so I became a Methodist local preacher, with a desire to preach only the good news of the Gospel, which I did.

My favourite verse in the Bible is John 9:25 'One thing I know, that whereas I was blind, now I see.' That describes the change in me. Now I have the love of God in my heart.

I would like to thank Mr. Bent for writing to *Powerful Passages*. What he has said reminds me of something I read by Glen Hoddle, the international football player. He was to play for England against Israel in 1986. When there he visited Bethlehem and realised that something was missing from his life. After his conversion he was interviewed by *21 Century Christian*.

'It's like having shells taken off your eyes, if you like. It feels as if I've been walking around blind. Now I've only become aware of the true purpose of life, and what God wants us to do whilst we are here.'

Let us all thank the Lord for opening our eyes to see His way of salvation. Let us also ask the Lord to open the eyes of our heart, so that we may see more of the wonderful truths concerning Christ which are found in the Bible.

'I keep asking that the God of our Lord Jesus Christ, the glorious Father, may give you the Spirit of Wisdom and revelation, so that you may know him better. I pray also that the eyes of your heart may be enlightened in order that you may know the hope to which he has called you, the riches of his glorious inheritance in the saints, and his incomparably great power for us who believe.

"That power is like the working of his mighty strength, which he exerted in Christ when he raised him from the dead and seated him at his right hand in the heavenly realms, far above all rule and authority, power and dominion, and every title that can be given, not only in the present age, but also in the one to come.

'And God placed all things under his feet and appointed him to be head over everything for the church, which his body, the fullness of him who fills everything in every way.' (Ephesians 1:17-23).

John 11 and 12

The Raising of Lazarus

Cliff Richmond

This account of the death and raising to life of Lazarus contains many parallels with what God, through the Lord Jesus, does for Christians.

1) **Lazarus was loved by Jesus. 'Lord, the one you love is sick' (v3) and 'Jesus loved Martha and her sister and Lazarus' (v5).**

We see here that the love of Jesus is not confined to one person. Others are immediately included by the gospel writer. Earlier he had written, 'For God so loved the world that He gave His one and only Son' (3:16). And later, 'Greater love has no one that this, that one lay down his life for his friends' (15:13).

John explains this further in his first letter: "This is how God showed his love among us: He sent His one and only Son into the world that we might live through Him. This is love, not that we loved God, but that He loved us and sent His Son as an atoning sacrifice for our sins' (4:9-10).

If there had been only one sinner in the world, Christ would still have loved him and *died* for him.

2) **Lazarus was lifeless: 'Lazarus is dead' (v 14).**

Lazarus was, of course, dead physically and we all have to die sooner or later. As Solomon said, 'Like the fool, the wise man too must die' (Ecclesiastes 2:16).

However, before we accepted Christ as our Saviour we were dead spiritually as a result of our sins. As Paul reminds us in Ephesians 2:12; 'As for you, you were dead in your transgressions and sins in which you used to live when you followed the ways of this world.' Also Colossians 2:13: 'When you were dead in your sins and in the uncircumcision of your sinful nature.'

Lazarus was lifeless. So, too, were we.

3) **Lazarus received life through the Lord Jesus. 'The dead man came out' (v 44).**

The first thing a dead person needs is life, and this is the great theme of John's Gospel: (20:30-31).

John's use of the word life does not mean this present natural life which ends in death, but spiritual life which will be eternal. But this life is inherent only in Christ, but he is ready to give it to all who put their trust and faith in him.

'In him was life' (1:14) and 'Whoever believes in the Son has eternal life' (3:36).

4) **Lazarus received light. 'His hands and feet were wrapped with strips of linen, and a cloth around his face. Jesus said, "Take off the grave clothes"' (v 44).**

Before we found Christ it was as though we were in darkness. 'This is the verdict: Light has come into the world, but men loved darkness instead of light because their deeds were evil.

Everyone who does evil hates the light, and will not come into the light for fear that his deeds will be exposed. But whoever lives by the truth comes into the light, so that it may be seen plainly that what he has done has been through God' (3:19-21).

Like the blind man said when Jesus healed him, 'One think I do know I was blind but now I see.' This is the experience of those who put their faith and trust in the Lord Jesus Christ. (See *Powerful Pages* John 9:25) for a fuller treatment of this.

5) **Lazarus received liberty. 'Let him go' (v 44).**

Without Christ we are in bondage because sin makes slaves of us all. We are in bondage because no one has the power or ability to free himself. But what sinful man is *unable to do for himself,* Christ came to accomplish for him.

All that is needed is personal faith and trust in Christ's finished work. By these we find we are free from the bondage of sin. We have liberty. 'So if the Son set you free, you will be free indeed' (8:36).

Imagine, then, the old grave clothes to be the old sinful habits we had when we were spiritually dead. But habits are very difficult things to get rid of. Even the word seems to stick.

> HABIT – take away H and you've still got A BIT. Take away A – there still is BIT. Cut off B and you still have IT. Take away the I and you still have it to a T.

6) **Lazarus' new life was sustained. 'A dinner was given in Jesus honour. Martha served, while Lazarus was among those reclining at the table with Jesus' (12:2).**

We have a living Saviour who is always there. Whereas Lazarus, who was also raised, died again, the Lord Jesus is 'the living one: I was dead and behold I am alive again for ever and ever' (Revelation 1:18).

So whenever we need sustaining we can talk to him through prayer. We can have fellowship with him each day as we travel the pilgrim pathway. While our friends on earth may let us down, we know we can rely on the promises of the Lord Jesus and lean on him as Lazarus did.

7) **Lazarus's new life was manifested. 'On account of him many of the Jews were going over the Jesus and putting their faith in Him' (12:11).**

Christ gives us freedom, but we are not free to do what we like. Rather we are free to do what *he* likes. 'On account of him (Lazarus) many put their faith in Jesus' and this should be the effect upon others or anyone who has this new life which is found only in Christ. We should have a great influence wherever we are: at home, at work, at school.

'When we saw the courage of Peter and John and realised that they were unschooled, ordinary men, they were astonished and they took note that these men had been with Jesus' (Acts 4:13). It is the calling of us all so to walk that the world will take knowledge of us, that we have been with Jesus.

Acts 5:17-42

Cliff Richmond

There are certain verses in this passage which I would like to highlight as I think they will encourage believers to witness to their Lord and Saviour and be 'counted worthy of suffering disgrace for the Name.'

Verses 12-16 set the scene for the events which follow. It is because of the apostles' success, with more and more men and women believing in the Lord Jesus, that the high priest and his associates were filled with jealousy and had the apostles thrown into prison. However, they were not there long for through the miraculous intervention of an angel they were freed.

There is a parallel here with the miraculous way in which the Lord sets believers free from the power of sin: 'He has rescued us from the dominion of darkness and brought us into the kingdom of the Son he loves, in whom we have redemption, the forgiveness of sins' (Colossians 1:13-14).

At the open doors of the jail, the angels spoke to the apostles.

> 'Go, stand in the temple courts,' he said, 'and tell the people the full message of this new life.' (Acts 5:20)

I believe this command should be obeyed by Christians today. There is a desperate need that people be told 'the full message of this new life'.

The apostles wasted no time.

> At daybreak they entered the temple courts, as they had been told, and began to teach the people. (Acts 5:21)

We find examples of such immediate witnessing at the start of our Lord's ministry.

> The first thing Andrew did was to find his brother Simon and tell him, 'We have found the Messiah' (that is, the Christ). Then he brought Simon to Jesus. (John 1:41-42)

Then in verse 46, Philip says to Nathaniel 'Come and see.' Today there is an equal need for such urgency.

At the Open Bible Trust Conference held recently in Nottingham, Willie Henry, when dealing with the Christian's responsibilities to the world stated, 'Our primary responsibility is to communicate the good news about Jesus Christ to those around us, as the early apostles did.

Those apostles could not help speaking about what they had seen and heard (Acts 4:20). However, we should take note that preaching was not confined to the apostles.

> On that day a great persecution broke out against the church at Jerusalem, and all except the apostles were scattered throughout Judea and Samaria . . . Those who had been scattered preached the word wherever they went. (Acts 8:1-4)

Michael Penny, also speaking at the Nottingham Conference, said 'The church can fulfil its role in the world by having no ambiguity as to what constitutes the gospel and by stating it clearly.' Our yardstick for this is as follows:

'Now, brothers, I want to remind you of the gospel preached to you, which you have received and on which you have taken your stand. By this gospel you are saved if you hold firmly to the word I preached to you. Otherwise, you have believed in vain. For what I received I passed on to you **as of first importance**: that Christ died for our sins according to the Scriptures, that he was buried, that he was raised on the third day according to the Scriptures.' (1 Corinthians 15:1-4)

'I am astonished that you are so quickly deserting the one who called you by the grace of Christ and are turning to a different gospel – which is really no gospel at all. Evidentially some people are throwing you into confusion and trying to pervert the gospel of Christ. But even if we or an angel from heaven should preach a gospel other than the one we preached to you, let him be eternally condemned! As we have already said, so we now say again: if anybody, is preaching to you a gospel other than what you accepted, let him be eternally condemned.' (Galatians 1:6-9)

Returning to Acts 5, we find Peter and the apostles displaying a similar uncompromising attitude when placed before the Sanhedrin.

'We gave you strict orders not to teach in this name,' said the high priest. 'Yet you have filled Jerusalem with your teaching and are determined to make us guilty of this man's blood.' Peter and the other apostles replied: 'We must obey God rather than men!' (Acts 5:28-29)

Thankfully in the United Kingdom there are no laws forbidding the preaching and teaching of Christ and His message. That being the case, what holds back Christians from proclaiming the gospel today? Is it, perhaps that we are trying to do **God's** work in our **own** strength? I say this in the light of Gamaliel's words later in this chapter.

> 'Therefore, in the present case I advise you: Leave these men alone! Let them go! For if their purpose or activity is of human origin, it will fail. But if it is from God, you will not be able to stop these men.' (Acts 5:38-39)

The Sanhedrin were persuaded by Gamaliel and called in the apostles, flogged them, ordered them not to speak in the name of Jesus, and let them go. What was the apostles' reaction to being flogged?

> The apostles left the Sanhedrin, rejoicing they had been counted worthy of suffering disgrace for the Name. Day after Day, in the temple courts and from house to house, they never stopped teaching and proclaiming the good news that Jesus is the Christ. (Acts 5:41-42)

This incident could well have been in Peter's mind when he wrote his first letter.

> But in your hearts set apart Christ as Lord. Always be prepared to give an answer to everyone who asks you to give the reason for the hope that you have. But do this with gentleness and respect, keeping a clear conscience, so that those who speak maliciously against your good behaviour in Christ may be ashamed of their slander. It is better, if it is God's will, to suffer for doing good than for doing evil.

For Christ died for sins once and for all, the righteous for the unrighteous, to bring you to God. (1 Peter 3:15-18)

Let us, then, learn a lesson from Peter's experience in Acts 5 and from his letter. He taught the people. He filled Jerusalem with the teaching. Are we prepared to give an answer to everyone who asks about the hope we have in Christ? Remember what the Psalmist said.

Let the redeemed of the Lord say so.
(Psalm 107:2 KJV)

Romans 8:28

All things work together for good to them who love God

Michael Hughes

My father has been ill for some months and has recently had two spells in hospital. Just prior to his second visit he suffered a mild stroke and also got a kidney infection which left him somewhat disorientated.

In the early hours of Friday, January 27th he was rather restless. At 3:15 am he got up and decided he wanted to sit in his chair in the living room. Nothing I or my mother could do or say would persuade him to go back to bed. So we sat with him to make sure he was comfortable.

Several hours and numerous cups of tea later, I went to my bedroom to draw back the curtains and turn over my *Keswick Calendar*. The text for the day was Romans 8:28: 'All things work together for good to them that love God.'

> Each difficulty is met by a promise that guarantees that it can never become a disaster. The loving providence that governs the whole world will allow nothing to enter the life of a believer that is not for our ultimate good. (David Jackman)

What a comfort this text was in the early hours of that morning, at that time of domestic anxiety. It was very difficult for me to see any good in this particular situation, but here we have this wonderful promise: 'All things work together for good to them that love God.' *All things!*

Do we really believe it? Did I really believe it as I stood there in the grey light of dawn? Perhaps an experience like the one I am describing will help increase our faith.

Later that day my father was admitted to hospital, but has since been discharged and is now living in a private nursing home with my mother. He is as well as can be expected and for this, and for all God's goodness to us over these past few difficult months, we give Him all the thanks and praise.

1 Corinthians 15
The Resurrection
Cliff Richmond

His resurrection was foreknown

Firstly, in relation to our Lord, His resurrection was *foreknown*. There is no specific reference in the Old Testament, unless we count Job 19:25, 27, but there are types or pictures in various places.

On the third day of creation the dry ground appeared (Genesis 1:9-10). In Hosea 6:2 we read, 'After two days he will revive us, on the third day he will restore us, that we may live in his presence.' And, of course, the account of Jonah and the great fish about which our Lord spoke in Matthew 12 to give a sign to the Pharisees.

It was after this that He specifically told His disciples of His future death and resurrection (Matthew 16:21; 17:9), and promised resurrection to those who believed in Him (John 1:25-26).

His resurrection is a fact

Next we see that the Lord's resurrection was a fact. Why? Simply because the four gospels record it and their accounts are reliable.

Consider this, would these books, describing what had happened in living memory, have been accepted if the abnormal events were untrue? People are quite capable of recalling what happened thirty or more years ago and the gospel records would have been discredited had the resurrection not actually taken place. C. H. Welch lists the alternatives.

1) **Either they were telling lies, knowing they were lies;**
2) **Or they were telling lies in which they were sincerely deluded;**
3) **Or they were simply telling the honest truth.**

In 1 Corinthians 15:5-8 Paul cites some of the people who were witnesses to the risen Christ; Peter and the twelve, James and himself, and on one occasion over five hundred. Such is the evidence for the *fact* of the resurrection.

Resurrection is the foundation of the gospel

Thirdly, resurrection is the *foundation* of the Gospel (1 Corinthians 15:1-4; Romans 4:24-25). While it is important to stress the death of Christ as the one offering for sin, this is only half the gospel story. to put it bluntly, what use would be a dead Christ as a Saviour? (See Revelation 1:18; Hebrews 7:25). He is a *living* Saviour and consequently interested in each person and to Whom all shall, one day, give account (Romans 14:10-12).

Resurrection power has its basis in faith

Next, we see how resurrection power has its basis in *faith.* Abraham was promised that through his seed all the families of the earth would be blessed. However, he and Sarah had to wait until it seemed almost impossible for that to happen (Romans 4:16-21).

Isaac, the child or promise, was an example of resurrection power in operation, but this was not the only time in Abraham's life that he was to learn the greatness of that power.

The climax came when he was told to give back to God the son he has waited so long for. Why and how his faith stood the test is told in Hebrews 11:17-19 and Genesis 22:4-5.

We can learn much from this as we continue our Christian walk for we shall surely face trials and testings. When all goes well there does not seem to be a need for faith and trust in the Lord, but when the storms come we learn what sort of faith we possess and how much we are dependent on our God and Saviour.

As we read 2 Corinthians 11:23-27, we see what Paul had to go through. Now we may not have to endure all he did, but we know that whatever trial we may face, we can, in all things, be more than conquerors through the resurrection power of God.

Resurrection and the future

The idea of suffering for Christ leads us on to the *future*. The first letter of Peter and the letter of James were written to the dispersed Jews who were facing trials and persecution to encourage them to persevere, and reminding them of the glory which should follow.

The writings of Paul also indicate that there are rewards for faithful service (Hebrews 11:35; 2 Timothy2:12; Philippians 3:11, 14). This should encourage us to 'always give yourselves fully to the work of the Lord, because you know that your labour is not in vain' (1 Corinthians 15:58).

Whether we are prize winners or not, we can still look forward to that day when the Lord Jesus appears and we appear with Him in glory. Then we shall be raised to be ever with Him.

Hold fast to the truth of resurrection

Let us, then, hold fast to the truth of the truth of resurrection for 'if the dead be not raised, then Christ has not been raised either. And if Christ has not been raised your faith is futile, you are still in your sins. Then those also who have fallen asleep in Chris are lost' (1 Corinthians 15:16-18).

May our faith in the finished work of Christ on the Cross for our forgiveness and His resurrection for our justification enable us to be 'satisfied when I awake with thy likeness' (Romans 4:25; Psalms 17:15).

Ephesians 3:20-21

He is able!

Cliff Richmond

Now to Him who is able to do immeasurably more than all we ask or imagine, according to His power that is at work within us, to Him be glory in the Church and in Christ Jesus throughout all generations, for ever and ever. Amen.

In our previous article we considered the question 'How strong are we?' in the light of Ephesians 6:10-18 and 1:18-20. To this we can add Paul's testimony in Colossians 1:29.

> To this end I labour, struggling with all the energy he so powerfully works in me.

We see here that God is powerfully working in Paul just as 'His power is at work within us,' Ephesians 3:20. It is however, the beginning of this verse that I wish to examine.

What is God able to do for us?

First and most importantly He is able to save us (Hebrews 7:25). 'God did not send His son into the world to condemn the world but to save the world through Him' (John 3:17) and His Son, our Saviour, was called Jesus 'for He shall save His people from their sins' (Matthew 1:21).

Some examples from the scriptures of those who God saved are:

- **Despised Tax Collectors – Matthew and Zacchaeus;**
- **A woman taken in adultery;**
- **A dying thief;**
- **A sorcerer;**
- **A religious teacher – Nicodemus;**
- **The chief of sinners and persecutor of Christians – Paul;**
- **A jailer;**
- **A great multitude that no one could count from every nation, tribe, people and language.**

Having saved us God is also able to satisfy us. He 'is able to make all grace abound to you, so that in all things at all times, having all that you need, you will abound in every good work' (2 Corinthians 9:8). And verse 9, quoting Psalm 112:9, tells us that 'His righteousness endures forever.' God does not tire, as men do, in giving to His people.

Do we have Paul's assurance?

In satisfying us God is able to keep us even from falling (Jude 24) for, as 1 Peter 1:5 reminds us, it is 'through faith you are shielded by God's power.' Then, in 2 Timothy 1:12, Paul tells us that although he is suffering 'Yet I am not ashamed because I know whom I have believed and am convinced that He is able to guard that which I have entrusted to Him for that day.' Do we have such assurance? We certainly do!

First fruits

'That day' speaks of God being able to raise us up. In Hebrews 11:19 Abraham reasoned that God was able to raise the dead and we know this is exactly what He has done to the Lord Jesus for 'Christ has indeed been raised from the dead, the first fruits of those who have fallen asleep' (1 Corinthians 15:20).

So we can joyfully anticipate the time when this mortal shall put on immortality, when this corruptible shall put on incorruption, when death shall be swallowed up in victory (1 Corinthians 15:53-54). Then we shall have bodies like His own glorious body (Philippians 3:21). As Jude 24 continues, He is able 'to present you before His glorious presence without fault and with great joy.'

Ephesians 3:20-21 (Part 2)

He is able!

Cliff Richmond

We have already seen some of what God is able to do for us – to save, to satisfy, to keep, to raise, to present. However, the list is by no means exhaustive. We now focus on what God is able to do in us.

First, He is able to dwell in us: 'Know ye not that ye are the temple of God and that the Spirit of God dwelleth in you?' (1 Corinthians 3:16).

The word *dwell* means to use or have as a house. At gospel meetings I recall that often our salvation was spoken of as 'letting Jesus come into your heart,' where the heart is put for the whole being, the whole life. Paul's prayer in Ephesians 3:17 confirms that it is by faith that Christ dwells in our hearts and verse 16 says that we are 'strengthened with might by his spirit in the inner man.' This of course is what Christ promised in John 14:17: 'the Spirit of truth . . . dwelleth with you, and shall be in you.' Houses receive power from electric cables which reach every room. Similarly, we, as homes of Christ can be powered in all aspects of our Christian living by the Spirit of God.

Philippians 3:21 tells us that the Lord 'is able even to subdue all things unto himself.' If Christ is reigning within us then the enemies within, including the old nature, will be subdued. He will enable us to keep in control the fiery temper, the hasty tongue and many other things which offend our Lord and our fellow men. Nevertheless there will be times when the believer faces temptation, but being in fellowship with Christ means that we can be helped through 'for in that he himself hath suffered being tempted, he is able to succor (help) them that are tempted' (Hebrews 2:18).

We know too that when all forsake us He stands with us and strengthens us (2 Timothy 4:1) and a sense of His presence will inspire us. As believers we are expected to 'grow up into him in all things' and become mature Christians as we 'come into the knowledge of the Son of God unto a perfect man, unto the measure of the stature of the fulness of Christ' (Ephesians 4:14, 15). If our maturity depends on our knowledge of the Son of God then clearly study of the word of God is important and is commended by Paul because it is able to build up the believers (Acts 20:31).

Finally, let us remember that as we seek to serve our Saviour and Lord, He is working in us that which is well pleasing in His sight (Hebrews 13:31) and greater is He that is in us than he that is in the world (1 John 4:4). It is also worth bearing in mind that He is shut out from the hearts of the ungodly but dwells in whoever shall confess that Jesus is the Son of God (1 John 4:15).

Ephesians 6:10-18

How strong are we?

Cliff Richmond

Samson received great strength from the Lord because he was a Nazarite, set apart to God from birth. No razor was used on his head and his adherence to the Nazarite vow gave him physical strength.

While we cannot possess the physical strength of Samson, nevertheless, Paul exhorts us in verse 10 to 'be strong in the Lord and in his mighty power.'

In Colossians 1:11 he prayed that his fellow Christians would 'be strengthened with all power according to his glorious might.' This prayer is linked to his prayer of Ephesians 1:18-20; "That you may know . . . his incomparably great power for us who believe. That power is like the working of his mighty strength, which he exerted in Christ when he raised him from the dead and seated him at his right hand in the heavenly realms."

The important Greek words to note in these passages are *dunamis* (power), *iskus* (strength), and *kratos* (might).

Dunamis stands out particularly as it has been brought over into English in the word 'dynamite,' and this may help us see what power Paul is talking about. This dynamic power belongs to the nature of God and he is the source of power. 'We have this treasure in jars of clay to show that this all – surpassing power is from God and not from us' (2 Corinthians 4:7; see also Jeremiah 32:17).

Iskus is strength possessed or received and is linked with service and the most important commandment. 'Love the Lord your God with all your heart and with all your soul and with all your strength' (Mark 12:31; see also 1 Peter 4:11).

Kratos, might, means the exercising of strength or power, put forth with effect. On account of might, authority is obtained and exercised. Now the power of God operated in Christ during his earthly ministry (Acts 2:22), and in believers in the Acts period (Hebrews 2:4). They were given strength by which God shewed his might. They had the ability to perform miracles, even to raise the dead. But what of believers today?

Back to Ephesians 6:10-11; 'Be empowered (*dunamis*) in the Lord and in the might (*kratos*) of his strength (*iskus*). Put on the full armour of God so that you can take your stand against the devil's schemes.'

Our Lord warned the people of his day that in addition to his blessings, a child of God receives, there would be burdens. The joy of the Lord would be accompanied by the jeering of the world and the peace of God would be realised in the midst of persecution. We need to lay hold on the resources of heaven – the armour of God – for the strength to live lives worthy of our calling.

In 1 Samuel 17:38-39 David is about to face Goliath, the champion of the Philistines. Saul had said, 'Go, and the Lord be with you.' But then he proceeded to dress David in his own armour, which was all wrong for David who said, 'I cannot go in these!'

Do we waste time trying on someone else's armour when we should be equipping ourselves with the whole armour of God? Only in his armour will we 'be strong in the Lord and in his mighty power.'

Colossians 3:17

Cliff Richmond

If I were to write a book on some aspect of the Bible, the subject I would choose would be *Practical Christianity in the New Testament Letters.*

Both *Search* magazine and the booklets published by the Open Bible Trust have dealt with several of the epistles which abound in teaching concerned with living the Christian life; e.g. James, John and Philippians.

In his booklet, *Practical Christianity*, James Poole gave a summary to help the Christian who desires to please the Lord in his practical life. This he did under the heading of seven relationships; towards God, members of the Body of Christ, our family, people at work, the state, our enemies and all mankind.

From this alone it can be seen that we are dealing with a vast subject, yet at a recent family service the minister displayed on an overhead projector one verse which seemed to contain all we need to know about *practical Christianity.*

> Everything you do or say, then should be done in the name of the Lord Jesus, as you give thanks through him to God the Father. (Colossians 3:17 TEV)

The test to be applied to everything we do or say is that it should be done in the name of the Lord Jesus.

In *Search* 31 Michael Penny, when considering John 14:13, put forward an answer to the question 'What did Christ mean when He told them about asking *in my name*?'

> To ask in Christ's name means to ask with the intention that my prayer should be that of Christ if He were here now.
> (Metropolitan Anthony, Jesus Then and Now).

Applying this to Colossians 3:17 means that whatever we do or say should be the actions and words of the Lord Jesus Christ if he were here in our place. 1 John 2:6 agrees with this interpretation; 'Whoever claims to live in Him must walk as Jesus did.'

In the book *Learning and Living the Christian Life* by John Blanchard, which I reviewed in an early edition of *Search*, we are advised:

> If a thing is right, do it; if it is wrong, avoid. That is not very spectacular, but it is infallibly effective.

But what is right or wrong? Or let's put it another way – if the Lord was here in my place would he do this or say that?

There is more help in Colossians 3:16 which tells us to 'Let the word of Christ dwell in you richly.' John Blanchard says:

> God's word contains everything that a person need know to guide him into a holy happy and helpful Christian life.

Thus the more we study the Bible, the more we should know the ways we should act to please Him, and it should become more natural for us to act in those ways.

The words of Katie Barclay Wilkinson's hymn makes an excellent prayer as we meditate upon the points raised above and realise how often we fall short.

May the mind of Christ my Saviour
Live in me from day to day,
By His love and power controlling
All I do and say.

May the Word of God dwell richly
In my heart from hour to hour,
So that all may see I triumph
Only through His power.

2 Timothy 3:16-17

Cliff Richmond

All Scripture is God-breathed and is useful for teaching, rebuking, correcting and training in righteousness, so that the man of God may be thoroughly equipped for every good work.

I am sure that Paul's statement is both familiar to our readers and acknowledged in their hearts and lives. However, I do feel that although all is useful to us, certain passages will have a bigger impact upon us than others. I would like to share with you some examples of what I have read myself or have heard read in church, but each time the effect upon me can only be described as electric.

'When the seventh month came and the Israelites had settled in their towns, all the people assembled as one man in the square before the Water Gate. They told Ezra the Scribe to bring out the Book of the Law of Moses, which the Lord had commanded for Israel. So on the first day of the seventh month, Ezra the priest brought the Law before the assembly, which was made up of men and women and all who were able to understand.

He read it aloud from day-break till noon as he faced the square before the Water Gate in the presence of the men, women and others who could understand. And all the people listened attentively to the Book of the Law. Ezra the scribe stood on a high wooden platform built for the occasion.

Beside him on his right stood Mattithiah, Shema, Anaiah, Uriah, Hilkiah and Maaseiah, and on his left were Pedaiah, Mishael, Malkijah, Hashum, Hashbaddanah, Zechariah and Meshullam. Ezra opened the book. All the people could see him because he was standing above them, and as he opened it, the people all stood up.

Ezra praised the Lord, the great God; and all the people lifted their hands and responded, 'Amen! Amen!' Then they bowed down and worshipped the Lord with their faces to the ground.

The Levites – Jeshua, Bani, Sherebiah, Jamn, Akkub, Shabbethai, Hodiah, Maaseiah, Kelita, Azariah, Jozabad, Hanan and Pelaiah – instructed the people in the Law while the people were standing there. They read from the Book of the Law of God, making it clear and giving the meaning so that the people could understand what was being read'
(Nehemiah 8:1-8).

What an occasion! All the people assembled as one man and they actually told Ezra to bring out the Law of Moses! Then he read it to them – not just a few verses, but from daybreak till noon, and they listened attentively.

What a privilege for Ezra to praise the Lord, the Great God, and to hear a resounding 'Amen! Amen!' The Lord and His written word were given their rightful place.

The finale of this passage has the Levites reading from the Law and instructing the people so that they could understand what was being read – an example that some modern-day preachers and teachers would do well to follow.

a powerful passage? What do you think? Do let us know. In future issues I hope to bring more examples of my own, but would welcome your thoughts on any verses from the Bible which have made an impression on you.

1 Peter 1:3-5

John Diamond

Praise be to the God and Father of our Lord Jesus Christ! In His great mercy he has given us new birth into a living hope through the resurrection of Jesus Christ from the dead and into an inheritance that can never perish, spoil or fade – kept in heaven for you, who through faith are shielded by God's power until the coming of the salvation that is ready to be revealed in the last time.

This passage appeals to me because of the invigorating confidence that is revealed in it by the resurrection of the Lord Jesus Christ. Not only Peter, but all the apostles and disciples of Jesus had this confidence as well as joy, when they realised that God had raised up Jesus from the dead. We, too, should rejoice (verse 6) when we grasp this truth with assurance.

Peter was a man among many who had lost his hope or, more correctly, had a misplaced hope. He, with others, had hoped that Jesus was going to bring in God's Kingdom on earth in their lifetime.

All the disciples, including the two on the Emmaus road, had been disappointed at the death of Jesus, and were very despondent, none more so than Peter.

Peter went so far as to deny any allegiance at the time of the trial of Jesus, but after the resurrection of the Lord Jesus Christ, how his attitude changed. He was revived to a living hope. This was true of all the disciples and apostles.

Peter now speaks with cheerful confidence and assertion in these opening words of his epistle. Speaking in the plural he includes all 'God's elect,' and says they now have 'a living Hope,' because of the resurrection of Jesus Christ.

'Without resurrection our preaching is in vain'

I believe the resurrection is *the* most important tenet of the Christian faith. Even the death and cross of Christ has little value without it, being vindicated by the resurrection, as 1 Corinthians 15 asserts. Without resurrection our preaching is vain – hopeless (1 Corinthians 15:14).

After Christ's resurrection all the apostles were willing to suffer and die because of this hope, which had been revived in them.

Hope in the resurrection was evident in the Old Testament. For example, Job, in the midst of all his trouble, had this hope: 'I know that my Redeemer lives and that in the end He shall stand on the earth. And after my skin has been destroyed, yet in my flesh will I see God' (Job 19:25-26).

Abraham, in his stress and anguish, rejoiced to see the Lord's day, the day of resurrection. He reasoned God could raise the dead (Hebrews 11:1, 17-19).

In the middle of Lamentations (3:16-33) that hope is expressed and contains words that Peter himself might have spoken. This hope is seen in Ezekiel 37:11-14.

Martha, in her bereavement, knew that Lazarus would rise at the last day (John 11:24). A hope in resurrection based in the Old Testament Scriptures. And Peter refers to those Old Testament Scriptures when he tells the people what God had done by raising this Jesus of Nazareth – see Acts 2:22-32 and note verses 26-27 and cf. Psalm 16:8-11.

Paul had this hope in mind when he stood on trial before the Sanhedrin (Acts 23:6), before Felix (24:15) and before Agrippa (26:6-8). This was the hope of Israel but Gentiles, too, have this living hope because of the resurrection of Jesus Christ.

'Our hope goes beyond resurrection'

In fact, our hope goes beyond resurrection, taking in ascension, as revealed by Paul in the opening verses of Ephesians and also 2:4-7:

> 'But because of his great love for us, God, who is rich in mercy, made us alive with Christ even when we were dead in transgressions – it is by grace you have been saved. And God raised us up with Christ and seated us with Him in the heavenly realms in Christ Jesus, in order that in the coming ages he might show the incomparable riches of his grace expressed in his kindness to us in Christ Jesus.'

This hope brought forth worship and great praise from Paul, as it should from all of us.

The very gospel, itself, is based on this hope promised beforehand through the prophets (Romans 1:1-4) and promised before the beginning of time (Titus 1:2). Believing this hope gives assurance of salvation (Romans 10:9).

Why had this hope lapsed among the followers of Jesus at the time of His death? Why hadn't they seen in Jesus the fulfilment of God's promises and will? Was it because of a misplaced hope?

Many Christians hope for Utopia, paradise or the Kingdom of God on earth this side of resurrection and Christ's return. Have they, like Peter and the other disciples before Christ's resurrection, got a misplaced hope?

Perhaps we should realise, as Peter goes on to say, we can expect only trials and sufferings until 'the Lord's day.' Human efforts will not achieve a paradise on earth. That comes when Christ returns and resurrection occurs.

Peter, in this *powerful passage* has a living hope based on resurrection. Have we?

1 John 5:20

Eternal life's reality

Rowland Wickes

We know the Son of God has come and has given us understanding, so that we may know Him who is true. And we are in Him who is true – even in His Son Jesus Christ. He is the true God and eternal life

There are passages in Scripture which tell us about:

The gift of eternal life	The hope of eternal life
The promise of eternal life	Possessing eternal life
Inheriting eternal life	Laying hold of eternal life

All these aspects express the Christian believer's relationship to that life. The wonder of this verse in the first epistle of John is that it expresses rather the intrinsic character of eternal life, the tokens of the presence in the believer's life and the experience of its reality in the believer's heart. we find from this verse moreover that it is so centred in the Lord Jesus Christ, that it is the experience of *His* reality which comes through to us.

It begins with a historical fact; 'We know (we are aware) that the Son of God has come.' However, it goes on to tell of something beyond awareness, namely that He 'has given us an understanding.' This is where reality steps in; our understanding is awakened. The Holy Spirit makes this effective. The Lord Himself said, as he recorded in John 15:26, 'He will testify of me.' The Spirit of God is the Spirit of wisdom, of knowledge and of understanding. Through His gracious work we as believers begin and go on to know the Lord, not just to know about Him.

Then we are told that this One Whom we have come to know is to be embraced as 'Him Who is true.' New testament Greek has two words for 'true' or 'truth;' one *factual* truth as opposed to a lie, and the other *genuine* truth as opposed to that which is spurious. The word in this verse is the latter: in other words we could render the phrase, 'Him Who is genuine' or Him Who is real.'

Now in John 17:3 the Lord in His prayer to His Father uttered these words: 'Now this is eternal life, that they may know you, the only true God, and Jesus Christ, Whom You have sent.' This verse of itself could be construed as saying that our Lord is just the servant who passes on the life of God to His people.

However, when we proceed in 1 John 5:20 we find in addition to our knowing 'Him who is true' we are found to be 'in Him Who is true.' Then we see that this One Who is true is God's Son, Jesus Christ, for it says, 'even in His Son Jesus Christ.' Not only do we have here the identification of the believer with the Lord Jesus Christ, but we discover that 'He is true God and eternal life.' So we are told two things which are inseparable concerning our Lord. He is the true God and He is also our eternal life.

This is what the Holy Spirit's gift of understanding brings to us, the experience of the reality of Who Jesus Christ is and with that the realisation that this life is in God and in Jesus Christ. All this is something we get to know by the Spirit's help in the word of God. Perhaps we could justifiably express this verse as follows: 'We are aware that the Son of God has come and that He has granted us a spiritual understanding, so that we may get to know

Him Who is real. And we are in Him Who is real – even His Son Jesus Christ. He is the real God and eternal life.'

The heart bows in worship at this precious revelation of truth, because this truth becomes a real and living thing. It is no wonder that the next and final verse of this epistle says, 'Dear children, keep yourselves from idols.'

Doxologies!

Cliff Richmond

I began this series in *Search* 30 by considering Nehemiah 8:1-8 and commented upon verse 6, 'What a privilege for Ezra to praise the Lord, the great God, and to hear a resounding *'Amen! Amen!'*

There are many verses in the New Testament letters, termed *doxologies*, where the writers give glory to God. I would like to place some of these before you, for I find them *powerful passages* which show me how and teach me why I should praise the Lord.

Paul habitually prayed for the needs of his readers and often for his own needs too. He knew the Lord was able to meet those needs and, because of this, he gave Him praise and glory.

> "Now to Him who is able to do immeasurably more than all we ask or imagine, according to His power that is at work within us, to Him be glory in the church and in Christ Jesus throughout all generations for ever and ever! Amen." (Ephesians 3:20-21; see also Philippians 4:18-29 and 2 Timothy 4:18)

Peter and Jude wrote in a similar manner.

> "And the God of grace, who called you to his eternal glory in Christ, after you have suffered a little while, will Himself restore you and make you strong, firm and steadfast. To Him be the power for ever and ever. Amen." (1 Peter 5:10-11; see also 4:11)

"To him who is able to keep you from falling and to present you before his glorious presence without fault and with great joy – to the only God our Savior be glory, majesty, power and authority, through Jesus Christ our Lord, before all ages, now and for evermore!" Amen. (Jude 24)

As well as God providing us with strength for living the Christian life, Paul reminds us that He is also rich in mercy. In Romans 11 he tells us that 'All Israel will be saved . . . for God's gifts and His call are irrevocable.' This leads him on to write stupendous words about God.

"Oh, the depth of the riches of the wisdom and knowledge of God! How unsearchable His judgments, and His paths beyond tracing out! Who has known the mind of the Lord? Or who has been His counsellor? Who has ever given to God, that God should repay him? For from Him and through Him and to Him are all things. To Him be the glory for ever! Amen" (Romans 11:33-36)

But not only is God rich in mercy to Israel, he has also saved the worst of sinners and has rescued us from the present evil age.

"Here is a trustworthy saying that deserves full acceptance: Christ Jesus came into the world to save sinners – of whom, I am the worst. But for that very reason I was shown mercy so that in me, the worst of sinners, Christ Jesus might display His unlimited patience as an example for those who would believe on Him and receive eternal life. Now to the King eternal, immortal, invisible, the only God, be honour and glory for ever and ever. Amen." (1 Timothy 1:15-17)

"Grace and peace to you from God our Father and the Lord Jesus Christ, who gave Himself for our sins to rescue us from the present evil age, according to the will of our God and Father, to whom be glory for ever and ever. Amen." (Galatians 1:3-5)

Paul was constrained to praise the Lord when he reminded Timothy that Christ is to come again.

"I charge you to keep this commandment without spot or blame until the appearing of our Lord Jesus Christ, which God will bring about in His own time – God, the blessed and only Ruler, the King of kings and Lord of lords, who alone is immortal and who lives in unapproachable light, whom no one has seen or can see. To Him be honour and might for ever." (1 Timothy 6:14-16; see also Revelation 1:6-7)

The book of Revelation has many scenes which portray the worship of God for the salvation He has provided for His creation. For example, 4:11 and 7:10-12. However, for me the ultimate passage is 5:9-14.

And they sang a new song:

"You are worthy to take the scroll and to open the seals, because you were slain, and with your blood you purchased men for God from every tribe and language and people and nation. You have made them to be a kingdom and priests to serve our God, and they will reign on the earth."

Then I looked and heard the voice of many angels, numbering thousands upon thousands, and ten thousand times ten thousand. They encircled the throne and the living creatures and the elders. In a loud voice they sang:

"Worthy is the Lamb, who was slain, to receive power and wealth and wisdom and strength and honour and glory and praise!"

Then I heard every creature in heaven and on earth and on sea, and all that is in them, singing:

"To Him who sits on the throne and to the Lamb be praise and honour and glory and power, for ever and ever!"

The four living creatures said, "Amen," and the elders fell down and worshipped.

It is worth noting the buildup of voices engaged in the singing of this new song.

- Verses 9-10 have four living creatures and twenty-four elders.
- Verses 11-12 have many angels, thousands upon thousands, ten thousand times ten thousand.
- Verses 13-14 have every creature in heaven and on earth, under the earth and on the sea.

May we want to join that choir in singing that new song. May we take every opportunity to worship the Lord and to say that He is worthy. He was slain for our sins and by his blood He purchased us. Amen!

40 Problem Passages

If you have enjoyed reading these Powerful Passages you may well find Michael Penny's book *40 Problem Passages* of great help.

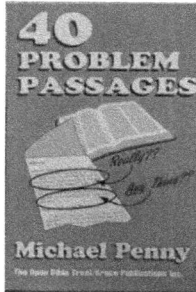

There are, of course, far more than 40 Problem Passages in the Bible. However, in this book Michael Penny not only solves these 40 Problem Passages, but in doing so he equips the reader with a method by which many, many more hard to understand and difficult passages can be understood and successfully applied to the life of the believer today.

Copies of the above book can be obtained from
www.obt.org.uk
and from

The Open Bible Trust
Fordland Mount, Upper Basildon,
Reading, RG8 8LU, UK.

It is also available as an eBook from Amazon and Apple
and as a paperback from Amazon.

About the editor

Michael Penny was born in Ebbw Vale, Gwent, Wales in 1943. He read Mathematics at the University of Reading before teaching for twelve years and becoming the Director of Mathematics and Business Studies at Queen Mary's College Basingstoke in Hampshire, England. In 1978 he entered Christian publishing, and in 1984 became the administrator of the Open Bible Trust, a position he held for seven years, before moving to the USA and becoming pastor of Grace Church in New Berlin, Wisconsin. He returned to Britain in 1999 and taught Maths at a Special School until 2004.

At present he is the editor and administrator of the Open Bible Trust. He has been chair of Churches Together in Reading for ten years, Chair of Churches Together in Berkshire for one year, and has been on the Advisory Committee to Reading University Christian Union for eight. He is lead chaplain at Reading College and is Head Chaplain for Activate Learning Colleges including the City of Oxford College, Banbury College, Blackbird Leys College and Bracknell and Wokingham College. He has appeared on Premier Radio and BBC Radio Berks on many occasions. He has an itinerant ministry which takes him into churches of different denominations.

In 2019 the Bishop of Reading nominated him to receive the Maundy Money from the Queen for his services to Christianity, the Church and the Community and he was one of the 93 men selected by Buckingham Palace from across the United Kingdom, along with 93 women.

Some of the major works written by Michael Penny,
published by The Open Bible Trust include:

40 Problem Passages
Approaching the Bible
The Bible! Myth or Message?
Galatians: Interpretation and Application
Joel's Prophecy: Past and Future
The Miracles of the Apostles
Paul: A Missionary of Genius
James: His life and letter
Peter: His life and letters
Comments and Queries about Christianity
Comments and Queries about the New Testament
Introducing God's Plan (with Sylvia Penny)
Introducing God's Word (with Carol Brown and Lynn Mrotek)
Following Philippians (with W M Henry)
The Will of God: Past and Present (with W M Henry)
Abraham and his seed (with Sylvia Penny and W M Henry)

He has also written a number of study guides including:
Moving through Mark
Learning from Luke
The Manual on the Gospel of John
Going through Galatians
Exploring Ephesians
A Study Guide to Psalm 119
The Balanced Christian Life (Ephesians)
Search the Acts of the Apostles (with Neville Stephens)

For a full list, and for details of the above, please visit
www.obt.org.uk

Also by Michael Penny

Four good books on four great people

From the pen of Michael Penny

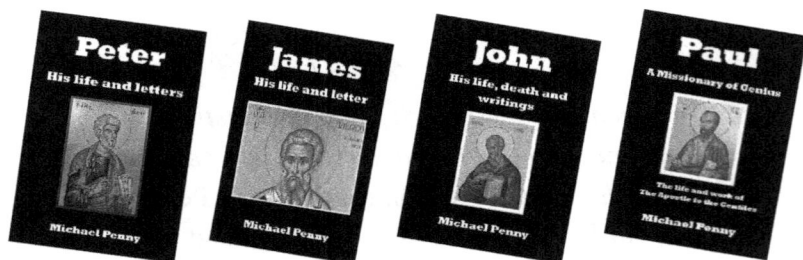

Peter: His life and letters
Peter! A solid rock or a moveable stone?

When did Peter first appear on the scene? What was he like as a person? What were his strengths and weaknesses? And what were the highs and lows of his life?

He denied Christ but became the immoveable force in the years following Christ's death, resurrection and ascension, but what happened to him after that?

This is a comprehensive and sympathetic treatment of one of the most important men in the New Testament, a person we all can identify with and learn from.

James: His life and letter

This book opens with an excellent portrait of James, who did not believe in Christ when He was on earth, yet who rose to be head of the Jerusalem Church. Then follows a section dealing with the dating of James. The greater part of the book is a clear and useful commentary on the letter, while the concluding section has helpful appendices dealing with (1) unanswered prayer, (2) why James thought it was the last days and (3) why he expected Christ to return soon.

John: His life, death and writings

Peter stands out from amongst the Twelve, being willing to speak and act when others lay silent and still. He was the natural leader and was dominant in the witness to Jews following Christ's resurrection. During those early years Peter was often accompanied by John, who seems to have been his right-hand man, his main support and ally.

This book lays before the reader what the Scriptures have to say about John in chronological order. It also gives an overview of each of his writings and deals with many of the questions and queries some people have. For example … Was John the disciple whom Jesus loved? Did he write the Fourth Gospel? Did he die of old age in Ephesus?

Paul: A Missionary of Genius
The life and work of The Apostle to the Gentiles

"One good reason why Christianity was triumphant was that it found in Saul of Tarsus, later St. Paul, a missionary of genius … Though himself a Jew, Paul took this new and startling religion out of Judaism into the world of the Gentiles," wrote the novelist J B Priestley.

But what do we know about this man Saul, who became Paul? This book covers all his life; from Pharisee to Christian, from Tarsus to Jerusalem, from Antioch to Rome. It also covers his diverse teaching; explaining clearly his two-fold commission to go to the Gentiles as well as Jews, and his later ministry when such distinctions became irrelevant.

Copies of the books on the previous can be obtained from

www.obt.org.uk

and from

The Open Bible Trust
Fordland Mount, Upper Basildon,
Reading, RG8 8LU, UK.

They are also available as eBooks from Amazon and Apple and as paperbacks from Amazon.

Publications of The Open Bible Trust must be in accordance with its evangelical, fundamental and dispensational basis. However, beyond this minimum, writers are free to express whatever beliefs they may have as their own understanding, provided that the aim in so doing is to further the object of The Open Bible Trust. A copy of the doctrinal basis is available on **www.obt.org.uk** or from:

THE OPEN BIBLE TRUST
Fordland Mount, Upper Basildon,
Reading, RG8 8LU, UK

www.ingramcontent.com/pod-product-compliance
Lightning Source LLC
Chambersburg PA
CBHW070550030426
42337CB00016B/2436